ST CHRIST
SCHOOL:
A SHORT HISTORY

Chris McNab

SHIRE PUBLICATIONS

Published in Great Britain in 2014 by Shire Publications Ltd,
PO Box 883, Oxford, OX1 9PL, UK
PO Box 3985, NewYork, NY 10185-3985, USA

E-mail: shire@shirebooks.co.uk   www.shirebooks.co.uk

A CIP catalogue record for this book is available from the
British Library.

ISBN-13: 978 0 74781 320 0
E-pub ISBN: 978 1 78442 045 1
PDF ISBN: 978 1 78442 046 8

Chris McNab has asserted his right under the Copyright,
Designs and Patents Act, 1988, to be identified as the
author of this book.

Editor: Ruth Sheppard
Indexer: Zoe Ross
Typeset in Perpetua Std and Gill Sans.
Printed in China throughWorldprint Ltd.

14 15 16 17 18 19   10 9 8 7 6 5 4 3 2 1

COVER IMAGE
Senior School. Despite the huge developments to
St Christopher over its lifetime, it has maintained its focus
on beautiful surroundings as a support for intellectual
activity.

TITLE PAGE IMAGE
Camp, 1938.

CONTENTS PAGE IMAGE
Children lining up to run a race in the early 1930s.

ACKNOWLEDGEMENTS
The author would like to thank Richard Palmer,
headmaster of St Christopher, for his support during the
research for this book. Special thanks also go to David
Cursons, secretary of the Old Scholars' Club, for his
invaluable guidance over many historical and factual issues.

The photographs are mainly reproduced from the
school's own collection. St Christopher would like to
thank Millicent Sutherland, Violet Cornforth, Helen
Soutar, Mary Muray, Kathleen King-Harris and Derek
Hill for photographs used here, which they donated
to the collection, and to Martin Brunt for donation of
photographs taken by his father, Donald Brunt. Thanks
also to JudithTaylor and RosemaryThorpe for the loan of
photographs reproduced here.

Shire Publications is supporting the Woodland Trust, the UK's leading woodland conservation charity, by funding the dedication of trees.

CONTENTS

FOREWORD

FOR ONE HUNDRED YEARS St Christopher School has provided a distinctive education for thousands of children. Reg Snell's book documented in some detail the early life of the school and the founders, who were clearly pioneers of their time. This book brings our story up to date.

Today the school thrives and successfully blends the preservation of childhood with preparation for life in a modern world. There is ever-growing pressure for children to 'grow up' too quickly and the school continues to resist this.

When young people leave St Christopher they do so ideally equipped for the modern world: creative, careful, compassionate and considered thinkers who value all people and who are open to change.

Parents, universities and employers constantly tell us that the qualities our leavers possess are more than just good academic results – they are qualities that will stand them in good stead for their role as leaders of the next generation.

At our last inspection the Lead Inspector wrote that the school does not let pride stifle innovation and I can think of no better accolade for a community that has evolved successfully over the past one hundred years and continues to do so.

Happy birthday St Chris, and many happy returns.

Richard Palmer
Head

Opposite: Twenty-first century building at St Christopher, designed by an Old Scholar and housing maths, IT and English classrooms. It is linked to the Sixth Form Centre.

Overleaf: A portrait photograph of Dr John Horace Armstrong Smith, the head between 1915 and 1918 of what became St Christopher School.

With much love from "the doctor"

FOUNDATIONS 1915–18

THEOSOPHY WAS, AND REMAINS, an arcane philosophy to the uninitiated. In its broadest terms, it explores the interaction between the physical universe, humanity and the divine. It therefore might seem an unlikely foundation for an educational institution, but in many ways its values, ideas and practitioners sowed the seeds of St Christopher School in Letchworth Garden City.

On 26 December 1912, George Arundale delivered a speech at the annual convention of the Theosophical Society in Adyar, India. Arundale was an influential theosophist and the head of the Central Hindu College at Benares, a fusion of responsibilities that produced an especially progressive vision of education. The topic of his speech was 'Education as Service', the theme making reference to the book *Education as Service* by Jiddu Krishnamurti, a young Indian lauded by the Theosophical Society as a future 'World Teacher'. Krishnamurti's book would become a conceptual foundation for much of the early educational development at St Christopher. The content of the speech struck a chord with many of the listeners attending from the United Kingdom, not least Ada Hope Russell Rea. Along with a group of other inspired signatories, Rea composed a letter to the Theosophical Society leadership in Britain asking for support in establishing 'a school definitely and openly on Theosophic lines'.

The idea was generally well received, and fundraising efforts began in earnest in 1913, under the leadership of theosophists Josephine and Sidney Ransom. An initial whip-round collection

Jiddu Krishnamurti, Indian mystic and philosopher, was connected to the life of St Christopher via the Theosophical Society.

Arundale, one of the landmark buildings of the St Christopher site, here seen as it was when taken over from Letchworth School in 1916.

of 8 guineas was an insufficient start, but then the project gathered the direct support of Annie Besant, president of the Theosophical Society in Adyar, and George Arundale himself. In early 1914, a twelve-man committee was established to oversee the financial and practical challenges of establishing the new school. Letchworth was the natural venue. Not only was it the home of several key committee members, including the Ransoms and Rea, it also had a significant theosophical local community, a fact that would oil the wheels of the school's foundation.

An appeal for funds eventually bore fruit, and two semi-detached houses (28 and 30 Broadwater Avenue) were found in Letchworth as the new school buildings. The school also received a skeleton staff of five, including the indomitable new headmaster, Dr John Horace Armstrong Smith. The Garden City Theosophical School opened on 20 January 1915, with fourteen pupils ready for a new style of education.

A school certificate for passing a spelling test, printed on the school press, issued by the 'Garden City Theosophical School' and signed by Armstrong Smith himself.

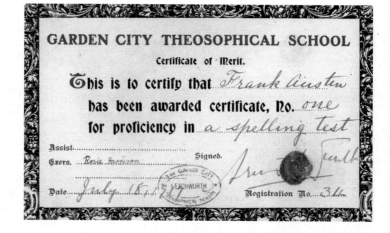

A Eurhythmics display by school girls in 1917. The eurhythmics dance/ exercise system was pioneered by Swiss musician Jaques-Dalcroze in c. 1905.

Armstrong Smith was a capable man to guide the school through its early years. He was a true internationalist, having worked at diverse locations around the world either as an educator or in medical service (he was a surgeon as well as a teacher). He was also a dedicated theosophist, and a man fundamentally dissatisfied with the rote-learning strategies and grim discipline that pervaded much of the British school system during the early twentieth century.

It is worth reflecting in some detail on the educational principles Armstrong Smith brought to the school in those early days, because in many ways they still inform the school today. Some aspects of school life were extremely forward-looking. On top of what Armstrong Smith called 'a sound general education', each child was encouraged to 'develop his own special talent' through subjects in which the child held a particular personal interest. In this way, education became a reward in itself. During teaching,

The school body at Arundale, a total of thirty-six pupils of the forty-one pupils on roll, assembled for the start of the autumn term in 1915.

9

St Christopher has had long associations with keeping poultry. Here, Dr Armstrong Smith and two industrious pupils keep watch over their flock.

children were allowed to take rest breaks within or outside the classroom, in order to refresh their concentration or focus. Discipline was largely self-imposed and there was no homework, as Armstrong Smith felt that 'you cannot do much with a tired pupil'. While it was accepted that the students would, eventually, have to participate in recognised public exam programmes, Smith boldly stated, when challenged about examinations by a visitor to the school:

> We shall have them when the children themselves wish to test their knowledge. And the results will not be publicly announced, but will be a private matter between teacher and pupil. In this way, we hope to do away with the spirit of competition, without destroying any of the keenness and stimulus to effort which an examination provides.

Other key principles of the school included a tolerant attitude to all races and religions, an emphasis on the spiritual benefits of beautiful, natural surroundings, a keen focus on physical health through sport and exercise, and a school diet that was (and remains) exclusively vegetarian. (For a few years parents could opt to give their children some meat, but this incurred an extra cost, and few took the option.) Under his jurisdiction, Armstrong Smith also encouraged the development of 'The Moot'. Founded on 25 November 1916, the Moot was initially a club formed by senior pupils. Over time, however, it began to accrue governing functions, debating and effectively legislating on school issues such as the care of library books or policies on bullying. In 1918 it was declared that 'the whole school is to be the Moot' – from now on, the pupil body in general was to have a significant influence in the running of the school.

THE RULES OF THE MOOT, 1918

1) Don't raise your voice in the house or classroom.
2) Obey without comment or discussion.
3) Don't contradict – everybody has the right to his opinion.
4) Say nothing unkind about anyone, whether true or untrue.
5) Don't interrupt – always listen courteously and patiently.
6) Don't exaggerate – be accurate in all your statements.
7) Play the game – neither grumble nor make excuses.
8) Our bodies must be kept scrupulously clean and tidy, so as to make the world more beautiful.
9) Our thoughts must be kept as scrupulously clean as our bodies.

Even today, the principles by which Armstrong Smith ran the school seem challenging and progressive. Many public figures took a keen interest in the new style of education, including the philosopher and broadcaster C. E. M. Joad, who observed that the teaching was founded 'not on the sameness of the children, their conformity to type, but on their differences.'

Smith acted as head until 1918, a period of three years in which the school grew both physically and educationally. A critical change came in the summer of 1915, when an injection of additional funding made possible the purchase of new premises at the top of Barrington Road. The building, which had formerly been a school, offered numerous benefits – extensive accommodation for boarders (up to forty pupils), a science laboratory, more classroom space, a playground and cricket field, and attractive gardens

The altar from Arundale chapel. Although the altar is Christian in imagery, St Christopher has largely avoided any sort of denominational religious affiliation.

The Cloisters, Letchworth Garden City.

and orchards. Relabelled 'Arundale School', these buildings would be the kernel of the school that exists today. The school also benefited from its relationship with the nearby Cloisters building – built by Quaker Miss Annie Jane Lawrence and run as an educational centre between 1907 and 1939 – the students utilising the swimming pool there.

A leaflet from c. 1919, showing various costs for Arundale day pupils, including transportation to Letchworth and Hitchin.

At the new premises, the school population grew fourfold, the epxanding pupil numbers fostering a new dynamism. Sport became an increasing feature of school life, the school fielding teams in hockey, cricket and athletics, and cultural societies were established and flourished, such as the Guild of Arts & Crafts and the Scientific Society. *The Arundale Magazine* appeared in autumn 1917, produced by the students and recording the latest school news and events.

There were also organisational changes. By March 1916 the school had been brought under the management of the Theosophical Educational Trust (TET), under which it remained for the next fourteen years. The trust enabled the expansion of the Barrington Road site, taking the total size of the school estate to 12½ acres. It also became more involved in the educational direction of the school, particularly through the expertise of one Beatrice Ensor. An experienced educator

ARUNDALE SCHOOL
TARIFF

For the week - end from Friday evening to Monday morning fifteen shillings

	s	d
Breakfast	1	— 6
Luncheon	2	— 0
Tea	1	— 0
Supper	1	— 6
Laundry	1	— 0
Traps to Letchworth station	1	— 0
Traps to Hitchin	2	— 6

and passionate theosophist, Ensor was appointed the trust's 'General Organizer' and advisor on educational development, and she would have a central role to play in the future of the school's development.

In late 1918, Armstrong Smith submitted his resignation from the headship of the school. The demands of running a new school during a time of war had taken their toll on his health, exacerbated by the crisis of caring for the many students affected by the Spanish flu pandemic that began in 1918. (At one point, all but two of the forty-two boarders were sick with the illness.) His resignation came as a blow to the trust directors, yet the school was established and thriving, thanks to the efforts of Armstrong Smith and his staff. What was important now was to take it into the future.

Opposite top: A postcard of the Cloisters, that most distinctive of buildings, which was used by early St Christopher pupils for its swimming facilities.

GUILD OF ARTS & CRAFTS.

CERTIFICATE OF MEMBERSHIP.

THE PRINCIPLES AND RULES.

THE OBJECT OF SEEKING MEMBERSHIP OF THE GUILD MUST BE TO SERVE BY EXPRESSING THE DIVINE IN ITS ASPECT OF THE BEAUTIFUL.

THIS PRINCIPLE MUST FIRST BE EXPRESSED IN UNFAILING COURTESY OF CONDUCT AND CLEANLINESS OF BODY.

MEMBERS MUST BE QUICK TO NOTICE AND TO REMEDY ANYTHING IN THE NATURE OF DISORDER.

MEMBERS MUST UNDERTAKE SOME SPECIFIC CRAFT OR ART WITH THE IMMEDIATE OBJECT OF BEAUTIFYING THE SCHOOL, AND MUST SATISFY THE MASTERS OF THE GUILD AS TO THEIR ABILITY TO ACCOMPLISH THE WORK.

THE MASTERS OF THE GUILD MUST BE SATISFIED TOO THAT THOSE WHO SEEK MEMBERSHIP CAN BE RELIED ON TO CARRY OUT THE WORK UNDERTAKEN AND TO LIVE UP TO THE PRINCIPLES.

THE ADMISSION FORM MUST BE SIGNED BY TWO GUILD MEMBERS.

PROMISE MUST BE SIGNED IN FULL MEETING OF THE GUILD.

I PROMISE TO ENDEAVOUR TO PRACTISE THE PRINCIPLES OF THE GUILD IN MY LIFE; TO KEEP THE HONOUR OF THE GUILD ALWAYS IN MIND AND TO WORK FOR THE SCHOOL BY

....

Signed: ....

Proposer: ....

Seconder: ....

An original membership certificate for the Guild of Arts & Crafts, the first of the guilds established in the school's history.

GROWING PAINS 1919–25

THE PERIOD FROM THE END OF World War I to the mid-1920s was a lively time in the history of St Christopher. Change affected every aspect of school life – leadership, finances, administration and intellectual growth. Ultimately, most of these changes were positive, as they introduced a fresh dynamism into school life.

The decade following the end of the war was a period of pronounced physical expansion at St Christopher. It should be noted that this expansion was conducted against a grim backdrop of financial struggles, as the world (and the school) lurched through a post-war economic depression. The TET in particular found itself overstretched by its commitments, a situation that would build up to the trust going into voluntary liquidation in 1932, by

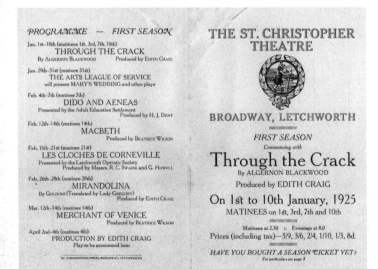

Opposite: Montessori pupils swimming in the pool at the Cloisters in July 1925.

Left: The programme for *Through the Crack*, the first play produced in the theatre when it opened in January 1925. The assistant stage manager of the show was none other than Laurence Olivier.

Annie Besant lays
the foundation
stone of the
Broadway buildings
on 25 September
1919.

which time St Christopher was thankfully in charge of its own finances. The
school was also directly affected by a general slump in the number of paying
boarders (only about thirty in 1923). Nevertheless, as physical developments
will show, the school still managed both to survive and to thrive.

Shaping young
minds – the
Brackenhill
Montessori group,
seen here in July
1920, probably in
the garden of the
Old Rectory.

A key priority for the trust in 1919 was to build a larger day-school site
separate from the boarding buildings. Two villas on Norton Way were rented
as the Modern School, previously (from 1912) the 'Modern School for
Girls' headed by a Miss Cartwright. The Modern School was led by Isabel

King (who was also a teacher of geometry at Arundale). Yet it was not a success, despite the formidable leadership. Thus Beatrice Ensor noted that the 'dwindling of the goodwill of the school through the leaving of a number of children when their parents removed from Letchworth after the Armistice, and the fact that the villas were proving most inconvenient, suggested the idea of building a suitable new day school.' The idea was accepted, and after much debate and disagreement the foundation stone of new school buildings at the junction of Spring Road and Broadway was laid on 25 September 1919. Pupils from Arundale and the Modern School moved into the new building in September 1920 (the official opening was 19 October). Arundale was now home to the boarders; the Broadway buildings were referred to as St Christopher, but they worked together as two parts of one establishment. The Broadway site, with its distinctive single-storey loggia front, included an assembly hall, which offered a useful space for everything from meetings to theatrical productions.

Another key development was that of the 'Brackenhill Home School', in Bromley, Kent, an institution that provided a safe and encouraging environment for war orphans and other disadvantaged children. The facility had its origins in a children's home, founded by feminist and suffragette Kate Harvey in the early war years, but it was transferred to the TET in April 1917. It was moved to the Old Rectory in Letchworth Lane in April 1920, where it could educate the children with greater convenience and through improved integration with the other Letchworth sites. The first class run specifically on Montessori principles also started at Arundale in the summer term 1920, and continued at Broadway, with Montessori-based education thriving to the present day in the Early Years Centre.

Brackenhill children outdoors, c. 1923.

Opposite top:
A characterful
photograph of
Isabel King, who
held a powerful
influence over St
Christopher until
her departure to
found Frensham
Heights.

Opposite below:
Beatrice Ensor was
a utopian thinker
and a passionate
educationalist,
and helped shape
St Christopher's
original values and
teaching.

The science
laboratory at
Broadway. The
teacher in the
background is
Mr Ernest N.
Fernyhough.

In 1923, it became clear that a rise in student numbers at the Broadway site (189 enrolments, although the school was only designed for 120) demanded significant expansion. Between 1922 and 1923 plans were drawn up, focusing on the addition of new classrooms, cloakrooms, storerooms, staffroom, sanctuary (effectively a non-denominational chapel), theatre and hall. The cost of all these features initially appeared prohibitive (£16,250, plus architect's fees), but benefactors stepped forward and the building work commenced. Thus by the autumn of 1923 the school was graced with considerably more educational space. The Junior School and Montessori Department each had their own dedicated space, while the theatre and new hall added greater space for group assembly (the latter also served as a gymnasium).

As this brief overview shows, St Christopher was a school community in a 'growth phase', a trend that seemed confirmed by the rise in pupil numbers at Broadway to 225, by the beginning of 1925. Yet a dramatic change was on the horizon.

It should be pointed out that by the beginning of the 1920s there were three principal educational establishments under the TET structure at Letchworth. There was the St Christopher School at Broadway, the Arundale boarding house, plus the Brackenhill charitable boarding house, which also sent pupils to St Christopher. The two great formative individuals presiding over these establishments were Beatrice Ensor and Isabel King, Ensor as a director of the TET and King as joint principal of St Christopher from September 1920. Sharing the principal role with King was Wilfred Layton,

also appointed to take charge of Arundale despite having no teaching experience. Following the charismatic Armstrong Smith would have been hard for anyone, but Layton seems to have not been particularly successful at guiding Arundale, although he did encourage school music, and an inspector who came in autumn 1920 recorded privately that 'he has no capacity whatever for class teaching'.

At Easter 1921 Layton resigned. Personal and professional issues were drawing him elsewhere (he would eventually become a priest in the Episcopal Church), and hence the TET had to fill the void. King was made sole principal of St Christopher, supported in an advisory capacity by part-time mathematics teacher Iwan Hawliczek and Ludwig Van der Straeten (known as Vandy), a talented arts and crafts master. Vandy was also appointed temporary principal of Arundale School in May 1921; it was still hoped that Armstrong Smith would return, but he was unable to do so on health grounds. Financial control of Arundale rested in the hands of Beatrice Ensor's husband, Captain Ensor.

Important school events of the early 1920s included the sale of a trust school at Grindleford (the Home School), and the transfer of the proceeds and the pupils into St Christopher. In 1922 the trust also applied to the Board of Education for official state recognition. A government inspection followed, which concluded ambiguously that the board 'were unable to place St Christopher School on the list of schools recognized as efficient [the term was used as a stepping stone to full recognition], but saw no reason why the standard required should not be reached later on.'

Vandy's resignation in the summer of 1922 saw his replacement by former Church

Mr Van der Straeten (known as Vandy), in this picture working as the arts and crafts master prior to his appointment as temporary principal, presiding over children at work in the art-craft room at Arundale.

of England vicar Frank Pigott. As well as being principal of Arundale House (the name was changed from Arundale School, to reflect that Arundale was now purely a school house for boarders), he also acted as vice-principal of St Christopher, alongside King. King herself remained emphatically in

Eurhythmics – a much photographed activity – 1920s.

charge, although overseen by the directors of the trust and aided by that force of nature, the 'Organising Director' Beatrice Ensor.

A real bombshell came in spring 1925, in the form of a letter from Beatrice Ensor in the quarterly Theosophical Society publication *Fellowship News*:

> For a variety of reasons, some of which are too complicated to enter into here, but partly because Miss King and I feel we cannot accept the policy of the Trust – and differences can occur in the best-regulated families! – but chiefly because we are both pioneers and feel the call to other work, Miss King and I are resigning from the work at Letchworth at the end of the summer term. We propose to establish another educational centre. As a result of our practical experience and of visits to most of the European pioneer schools, we have a very definite vision of the dream school which the particular development at Letchworth, and the nature of the district, do not enable us to carry out there.

The impact of the secession (for both the school and the trust) was heavy, however. The new school of Frensham Heights at Farnham, opened by Ensor and King, drew away large numbers of St Christopher boarders and day pupils – the various buildings of St Christopher experienced pupil

The St Christopher cricket team pose for a group photograph in the summer of 1921, with Vandy seen on the left.

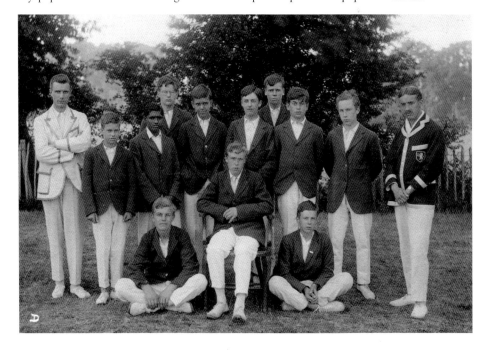

drops of between 25 and 50 per cent – plus nineteen members of staff. The school and trust now needed a new set of guiding hands to restore the school's confidence and direction.

The picture of St Christopher painted above is one of intellectual activity alongside administrative turbulence. Student societies of various kinds were founded and flourished. Alongside the Science Society and Guild of Arts & Crafts came the Dramatic Society, the French Society, the Music Society and a non-specific self-improvement club for boy boarders known as the Arundale Boot-lobby Club. School government was advanced with the foundation

There are many photos of the children 'messing about on the river' and enjoying themselves tremendously; this is an early example.

of the School Council during the first term at Broadway. The council consisted of thirty-two pupils (including all members of the Fifth and Sixth forms) plus staff and the principals, meeting on a fortnightly basis to discuss and legislate on school matters. King also initiated, in the spring of 1921, four games houses – Orange, Purple, Blue and White – although these were relatively short-lived and from 1927 until autumn 1943 there were just two houses, Green and Gold. She then proceeded to rearrange the system of forms, opting for 'Groups' instead. These Groups (numbered I to VI) were graded according to standards achieved, rather then purely by age, and students were given more control over their timetable and syllabus. Such changes were not implemented without controversy, but they nevertheless appeared to function.

The new theatre building, seating up to 600, was soon put to good work, as St Christopher began to lay the foundations of its long-standing dramatic excellence. The school hosted productions by pupils, local amateurs and professional companies, including Shakespeare's *Macbeth* and *The Merchant of Venice*, Purcell's *Dido and Aeneas*, Betty Jenkins' *More Things* and J. M. Barrie's *Pantaloon*.

FROM A SPEECH TO STUDENTS BY ANNIE
BESANT, ON A VISIT TO ST CHRISTOPHER,
16 OCTOBER 1925

If you *try* to be happy you will not be happy – but if you try to
make others happy, you yourself will become happy. Happiness is like
a butterfly – and it will not be caught unless you make others happy.
But you must not catch butterflies because that is cruel, but you can
catch happiness by being bright and joyous... If we keep our bodies
neat and clean and use them to help others – if we never think
thoughts of hatred but only of love – if we keep our minds clear, then
we are cleaning up the glasses so that the light can shine through.

Music, sport and creative arts all thrived under St Christopher's ethos,
but one particularly fascinating – and more commercially hard-edged –
phenomenon was the guilds. Essentially these were school artisan
organisations, dedicated to the practice of a specific art or craft. They
developed from groups of pupils formed to deliver practical services to the
Arundale community, such as printing, bicycle repair, small house repairs
and gardening. Yet the services were soon given a more enterprising focus

A St Christopher
production of J. M.
Barrie's *Pantaloon*,
produced in 1925
as part of a double
bill with *Land of
Heart's Desire* by
Yeats.

The library of the Broadway buildings, much in demand by the more inquisitive pupils of the school.

Members of the Tailoring Guild, hard at work making men's jackets for staff and students.

under the encouragement of Beatrice Ensor, who stated that an additional purpose of a guild was 'to produce certain commodities for the school below current prices, profits going to the enlargement and extension or any other purpose beneficial to the community, or of course of running expenses.' Here was a bold project, with groups of students running what were effectively miniature businesses. Ensor noted that 'Present activities include poultry, bee keeping, printing, photography; boot, cycle and other repairing, and confectionery. About 3,000 eggs and 90 lb. of pure honey have been supplied to the school.' The 'farming' activities referred to here were part of an agricultural scheme launched in autumn 1922, which also included the planting and maintenance of a fruit plantation. By autumn 1925, the school's agricultural scheme was occupying no fewer than 30 acres of land. Other established guilds included Weaving, Maintenance and Tailoring. During this year, however, the trust became concerned that the guilds had strayed well beyond their original goals, and had functionally become minor but largely unprofitable industries on school property. (The printing

guild was an exception – see below.) Most of the guild activities were therefore subsequently wound up, although they would return in later years.

One area of guild activity from this time deserves a special mention. This was the St Christopher Press, the school's very own printing house. *The Arundale Magazine* – the school's first in-house publication – was produced by students from late 1917 on a press lent to the school by a local Letchworth citizen. It ran every term for the first eight terms, until it mutated into the *St Christopher Magazine*. By this time the driving influence behind the St Christopher Press was one Vernon Booth, a St Christopher student who invested himself whole-heartedly in the print business. Following his completion of a four-year print apprenticeship after his schooling, Vernon became manager of the St Christopher Press in January 1924, printing for both the school and for outside agencies.

From this seed grew a printing business of considerable scale – by the 1960s it had fifty-five staff and had moved to separate premises in the town's industrial district. Times were changing, however, and the hard commercial realities of raising capital for investment saw the press sold to the Ladbroke's Group in 1968, under which it closed within months.

As we have seen, the period 1919–25 was a time of singular energy and event in St Christopher's history. Further great changes were on the horizon, not least changes of leadership and the onset of another world war.

The St Christopher camera club in action in the 1920s, a decade full of enthusiasm for the new art of photography.

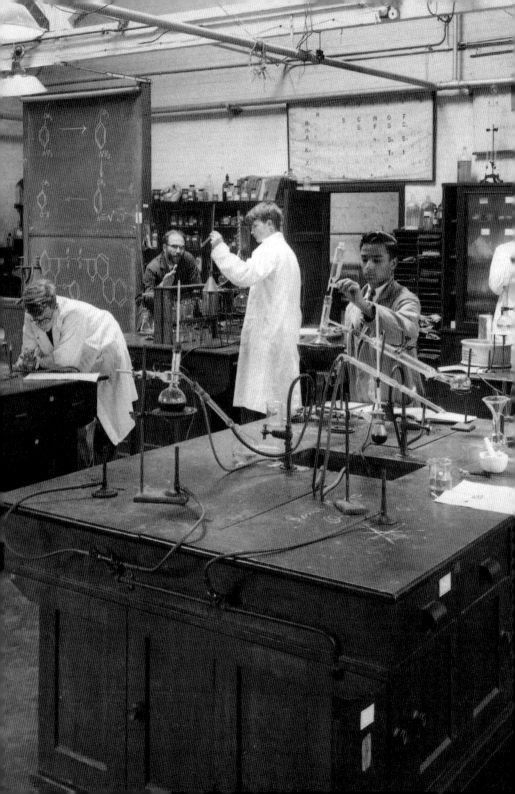

THROUGH WAR AND PEACE 1925–53

W ITH KING AND ENSOR GONE, Lyn Harris took over the role of the headship of St Christopher, aided by his capable wife Eleanor. Lyn would become one of the true formative influences over St Christopher, a man with vision and passion teamed to steely resolve. From the outset of his tenure, he had to face a challenge that threatened the very existence of the school.

The financial situation of St Christopher School in the second half of the 1920s was perilous in the extreme. First, in 1927 proposals emerged in Letchworth for a new 'Civic College', a secondary school that could have a major negative impact on St Christopher pupil numbers. There was a double threat here, as at this time St Christopher was actually making a loss, and it needed to increase, not decrease, student numbers just to reduce the level of annual deficit. Second, and more significant, was that donations from

Opposite: The lab at Arundale, in what became the library after 1956. The member of staff is R. G. Jones.

Left: An excellent photograph of Lyn Harris conducting outdoor pursuits with pupils in 1929.

long-term benefactors had dwindled, through the death of patrons and other causes. Money needed to be saved, and Harris proposed to the trust that the Broadway buildings be vacated and the buildings around Arundale and Old House (another name for what is today Arunwood) be developed to handle 150–175 pupils. Although the development work would involve financial outlay, this cost would be more than offset by the sale of Broadway.

The trust bought into the argument, and a letter was issued to parents in 1928 informing them of the changes. Two new wings were built on Arundale, and Harris was deeply involved in their planning, aiming to maximise space and light for each pupil. Although the move from Broadway took place in summer 1928, the trust struggled to find a buyer for the now empty building – it did not sell until 1934. Furthermore, the school was far from out of danger. To summarise a very involved issue, in 1928–29 the trust's financial crises continued, at a time when it also seemed to be losing its interest in funding education. Harris was informed that funds promised to turn the school round had been reduced dramatically, which would in turn undercut his plans to make the school self-supporting by 1931. The disagreements between Harris and the trust deepened, until in 1929 he tendered his resignation. This announcement brought a storm of protest from the Parents' Circle (effectively the country's first Parent-Teacher Association, formed at St Christopher in the early 1920s) and from former students. In response, the trust agreed to a new proposition from Harris – to purchase St Christopher outright, the business and buildings to be held by the St Christopher School Estate Ltd. It was a bold move, and one with considerable financial risk for the Harrises, but it held – the trust relinquished control of St Christopher

An aerial photograph of the school taken during the 1930s, showing the Senior and Junior Schools and two of the boarding houses.

and the school entered a new era. Lyn himself summed the age up in a publicity slogan: 'Education for the revolutionary world of tomorrow.'

The picture of Lyn Harris that emerges from the history of St Christopher is of a dynamic, thoughtful, energetic and enormously self-disciplined individual. Powerful characters can, in many settings, have a stultifying effect on the behaviour of those around them – especially the young – but Harris seems to have deftly steered around such rocks. What we see instead is a judicious mix of discipline and informality.

Lyn encouraged self-expression and self-government, but he also put in place structures to give the school anchors of time and behaviour. He introduced 'Service Time', fixed periods in the week when children would

The library at Arundale in the mid-1930s.

A notice of the suspension of the school's self-government after an incident during the summer term of 1932. Pupils had been shocked by a theft of money from a charity box. The school meeting passed a motion with an 'overwhelming majority' that Lyn Harris should be asked to interrogate all members of the school, and if that failed, the self-government of the school should be suspended until further notice.

The school orchestra performing before tea on Speech Day, July 1931.

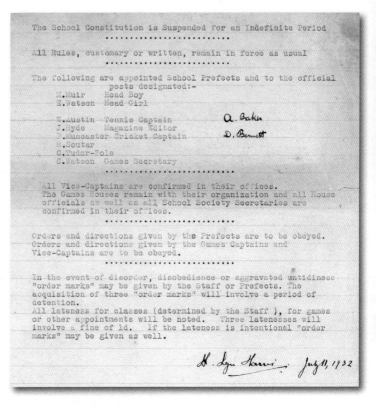

help the teachers perform school cleaning and maintenance duties. At Arundale, a time after breakfast was devoted to 'house work' (making beds, cleaning dormitories etc), and Harris maintained Layton's tradition of expecting the pupils to undergo the trauma of cold baths before their Morning Walk.

Yet such traditional rituals were more than balanced by Lyn's eye for freedom of thought and deed. He encouraged all forms of creativity, especially music and drama. The director of Music, Sidney Twemlow, instigated regular musical evenings, sometimes performed by visiting

Working outside, 1934. The man standing on the lawn is Christopher Buckley, who as a war correspondent for the *Daily Telegraph* would be killed during the Korean War. The teacher closest to the camera is Reginald Snell, author of a major school history published in 1975.

musicians and on many other occasions by musically talented pupils. St Christopher founded St Christopher Choral Society, a group of forty to fifty staff, students and parents, who gave good account of themselves in various operatic and choral productions.

Physical exercise is conducted in the school gym – the sides of the gym could be opened up to allow the free flow of air.

Canoe building,
1950s.

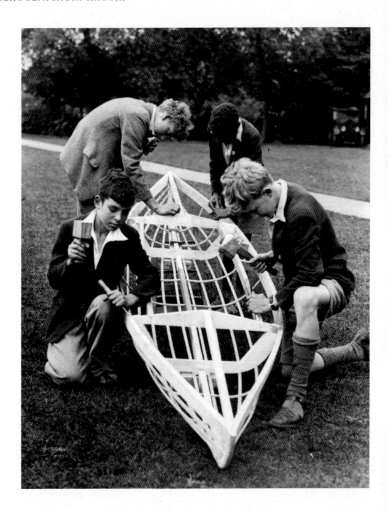

During this time the school fostered the spirit of the outdoor life, not only through sporting activities but also through simple adventures such as picnics and camping expeditions. For example, Eleanor Harris would on occasions drive a small group of seniors out to her family's log cabin in Burnham Beeches, for a weekend camp to prepare the students mentally for exams. Furthermore, in 1936 the school founded a travel scholarship, and students who utilised the fund travelled to places such as France, Belgium, Lapland, Moscow and Yugoslavia.

Lyn Harris maintained the emphasis on self-government by the school body, and some big decisions were made. In 1938, for example, school uniform for boys was abolished, following a 1,000-word protestation made in the school magazine. The girls' uniform was also subsequently dropped. (Although various forms of uniform had been adopted since the foundation of the school, in reality they had been somewhat inconsistently applied, as school photographs illustrate.) Yet Lyn insisted on mental rigour in every decision-making process. With forensic precision, he would spell out all the factors to be considered in a student debate, often resulting in the students making decisions that seem far more mature than their years would allow. Lyn also invested in the infrastructure of the school during the 1930s. He purchased several more buildings in the school vicinity for use by boarders and also rationalised dormitories to make them more private for the occupants.

Arunside camp, late 1930s.

The onset of World War II in September 1939 transformed the lives of all Britain's citizens and communities, and St Christopher was no exception. Air-raid practice was frequent and disciplined (the pupils had helped build an entire trench system at the edge of the playing field in 1938, complete with lavatories and electric lighting). The tedium of uneventful raid warnings, however, eventually resulted in the pupils staying indoors under Morrison shelters.

EXCERPT FROM THE EDITORIAL OF
ST CHRISTOPHER MAGAZINE, SUMMER 1940

Many schools have evacuated themselves to different parts of the country because of the war; we have not; and as yet we, or at least the children themselves, have felt the material discomforts and dangers of war very little. Only two air-raid warnings, one last September and one night raid this June, have been sounded here since the beginning of the war; food rationing is scarcely noticed in the school meals. We have felt some contact with the war, however, in that several of the children here have been, or are on the point of being sent to one or other of the Dominions.

St Christopher students during the war get to grips with the stirrup pump, probably in their role as fire-watchers.

The exigencies of war didn't exempt the Harrises from facing continued financial threats. There was the distinct possibility that the war would result in many parents withdrawing their children from the school, at the same time as the cost of living was rising. Staff salaries had to be reduced, and rather than impose a blanket low rate Harris had each staff member state the minimum he/she required to meet essential financial commitments.

As it turned out, student numbers did not collapse. Even in the second year of war, there were 247 pupils attending (132 boarders and 115 day pupils). By 1945, the last year of the war, the numbers had climbed still further, to 291. The growth in numbers was partly the result of those children who had been moved to 'safer' locations earlier in the war returning to the school in the later war years, as their parents felt more reassured about safety. War also provided, in its own way, opportunities for greater service and activity by the pupils. Many students attended agricultural work camps during the summer holidays. Traditional games

A MIDSUMMER NIGHT'S DREAM
By WILLIAM SHAKESPEARE

June 23 and 24 · 1939

Characters in order of speaking:

Theseus, Duke of Athens	Stephen Hall
Hippolyta, Queen of the Amazons	Dushka Howarth
Egeus	Jack Stubbs
Hermia (1st performance)	Toni Ogilvie
(2nd performance)	Nancy Robertshaw
Demetrius	Felix Leakey
Lysander	David Grensted
Helena (1st performance)	Monica Dorrington
(2nd performance)	Margaret Hingeley
Quince	Peter Talbott
Bottom	Nicholas Harris
Flute	Arthur Lloyd
Starveling	Allan West
Snout	David Masters
Snug	Derek Sayers
Puck (1st performance)	Philippa Hingeley
(2nd performance)	Helen Johnson
First Fairy (1st performance)	Pamela Wrinch Nicholson
(2nd performance)	Sheila Inglis

The cast list for *A Midsummer Night's Dream*, 1939. Note that Nicholas King Harris plays Bottom.

such as hockey and cricket were supplemented by ju-jitsu classes, for boys and for girls. The blacked-out gym was used for training in country dancing and ballroom dancing. Regular theatrical productions also defied the war's austerity, school productions including *Antigone* (1940), *Murder in the Cathedral* (1941), *The Immortal Hour* (1943) and *A Midsummer Night's Dream* (1943, by the Junior School).

Fittingly, when the war in Europe ended in May 1945 the school dissolved into celebration, with a two-day holiday characterised by picnics, bonfires and cheery renditions of *Auld Lang Syne*. Yet the legacy of the war was still felt across a devastated Europe, and the school rallied to various altruistic causes, such as fund-raising through a relief committee for the impoverished in Germany, Hungary, Greece and the Lebanon, plus war-damaged locations in Britain.

Some physical changes graced St Christopher in the immediate post-war period. In 1947, the Old House (renamed Arunwood) was bought back and used to house the Montessori Department and Housecraft, and the whole ground floor of Arunfield became the province of the Music Department.

By the early 1950s, the Harrises were veterans of St Christopher, having successfully guided the school through more than two decades. They decided, in 1953, that they should retire, effective from 1 January 1954. Yet they had no trouble finding a new custodian for the school – their son Nicholas would take over the headship.

Arundale is dramatically floodlit to celebrate VE Day in May 1945.

Overleaf: The St Christopher Recording Unit developed near-professional skills in audio recording techniques, recording dozens of news-style interviews during the 1960s. The team was filmed for the BBC *Tonight* programme in June 1960.

CHANGING TIMES 1954–80

A T THE POINT AT WHICH Nicholas King Harris took over the running of St Christopher, the school was about to enter its fourth decade of existence. As we have seen, each era of leadership brought its own character and developments, but also continuity. In short, St Christopher was developing strong traditions, but always centred around the same educational philosophy. The headship of Nicholas Harris brought with it further major changes in the school's history, but terminated in a tragedy that touched staff, students and old scholars alike.

Below: Nicholas King Harris and his wife Kathleen. His untimely death in 1980 was a tremendous blow to both staff and students.

There was no nepotism involved in Harris's appointment in 1954. Not only had Harris been a pupil at the school for thirteen years, but he also went on to have an exemplary academic and educational career elsewhere. His diverse posts held prior to 1954 included a youth leader in the Rhondda Valley, a welfare officer at a training centre for 'difficult' boys in Oxfordshire, and acting principal for the Brummana High School in the Lebanon. By the time he took over from his parents, he had also been running Arunside for three years. Thus there were few who could argue that he was not right for the job.

The Science Block, seen in 1961. This is the building after the completion of the first phase of development. Two more labs were added later in the decade.

Class taken by Reg Snell in the apple orchard outside the Science Block, after the first phase of building, 1960s.

A line of children pass bricks during the construction of St Christopher's swimming pool.

Senior girls sitting
out on the Las Gai
roof, sometime in
the years 1953–55.

Nicholas King Harris was a man of formidable energy, and nowhere is this better attested than by the building investment St Christopher received during his tenure. Indeed, space does not allow us to chart the full spectrum of the physical changes he brought to the school. The most comprehensive history (1915–75) of St Christopher, Reginald Snell's *St Christopher School 1915–1975*, notes that 'During the first seven years of Nicholas's Headmastership there are records of seventy-seven sizeable jobs of new buildings or improvements of existing facilities, forty of them in the Senior School and Arundale' (p.157). Examples of the developments included: a new science block, built in two phases during the 1960s to house biology, chemistry (both phase 1) and physics (phase 2); a new English classroom; additional Junior School classrooms; a new music school, further dining areas and kitchens; workshops and an arts and craft block; and a new accommodation building for senior girls, Las Gai, to name just some of the achievements. The school's library facilities were also developed and divided between a Reference Library, dedicated to formal academic research and reading, and a more informal Social Library, which held collections of fiction as well as being a place for lively discussions.

Yet the landmark construction of the 1960s was undoubtedly the swimming pool. The idea of an on-site swimming pool dated back to the 1920s, but it was Nicholas Harris who brought it to fruition. (The scheme was given extra momentum by the decision, in 1961, to fill in the Cloisters pool.) What was remarkable was the extent to which every stage of the pool's development and construction was a school affair. The project engineer was Stephen Harris, Nicholas' brother, who was not only Chairman of the Governors but also a Professor of Engineering at Cambridge. Parent and pupil committees raised the funds; building materials were begged and

The swimming pool
under construction.

borrowed. Moreover, the actual construction was performed substantially
by volunteer staff and students, who set up work rotas and residential work-
camps to ensure that construction kept going seven days a week, through
terms and holidays. When the pool finally opened in the summer of 1965, a
remarkable effort had been achieved, involving 250 tons of concrete and 30
tons of steel reinforcing. Snell notes that 'The total number of the labour
force over the three years of the pool's construction was in the neighbourhood
of 450, the age range being the five years of a Montessori child to Lyn
Harris's seventy-two years' (p.163).

'YOUTH' BY PIP WARWICK

Written for the *St Christopher Magazine*, summer 1960:

Sometimes I wonder who, or what I am,
What I was sent for.
And what is intended to be my place in life.
Pondering, I realise my place is
What I like to make it.
But suddenly, there is a huge barrier stopping me.
On inspection I find it to be fear –
Fear of myself and of my behaviour;
This barrier is so vast and invincible –
But I notice a small crack in it,
And slowly venture forth.
Peering through I see a wonderful spectacle;
I am perplexed and wonder what it means.
Suddenly I know;
It is my future –
If I am prepared to make the effort.

The end product – the swimming pool as completed in the 1960s. The students would have to wait until the 1970s for a high diving board, although this was later removed when the pool was covered during Colin Reid's headship.

Children of the Junior School work inside their newly refurbished classrooms in the early 1970s.

Students in the art room (now a biology lab) during the 1960s do some sketch work.

Alongside the physical changes between 1954 and 1980, Harris ensured that the best traditions of artistic, scientific and social endeavour continued at the school. The travel scholarships – suspended since the beginning of war in 1939 – were re-established, with students heading off to all manner of foreign fields, including Istanbul, Norway, Germany, Iceland and the French Pyrenees. Also undergoing something of a revival were the school's drama festivals. Some of these were truly ambitious affairs. One two-day festival involved no fewer than 110 actors and twenty-six stage staff, performing eleven plays. The school's actors staged all manner of plays throughout the school year, ranging from Shakespearean tragedies to modern light-hearted comedies.

Cookery at Arundale, c. 1967.

The traditions of school, local and international service were also running strong. Nicholas revived the lapsed practice of Service Time, previously performed only intermittently by the student Companies. (Companies were first formed in the early 1920s; they were, and remain, student advisory groups headed by a dedicated 'adviser'.) Nicholas, acting on a suggestion of the school's estate manager, Simon Harris, channelled

'French Day' in the summer of 1959 was organised by French teacher Derek Hill and featured a fashion show, the female students modelling continental styles of the day.

Service Time into three major projects: the construction of two hard tennis courts; the building of an open-air theatre in the Junior School grounds; and the levelling of a car park. After a sputtering start, the projects were eventually completed by student volunteers.

Volunteerism also showed altruistic tendencies amongst the student body. On 18 July 1978, for example, five members of staff and thirteen student 'helpers' brought twelve handicapped children aged between thirteen and eighteen from London to St Christopher for a week's Handicapped Children's Holiday, an activity that the school would continue to host for many years. The school magazine (still going strong as a mouthpiece for school events) noted that the week included 'taking them shopping in Letchworth, various games (including swimming when the weather permitted) and on Thursday we went to a Pantomime at Fearnhill school. The whole of Friday was spent at Woburn Safari Park, which (as expected) was the most expensive outing of the week.' The care also extended to other pupils within the school. The same magazine touchingly notes that 'In a long and sunny first half of term, Juniors enjoyed playing in our new sandpit, built for us by some Senior boys last term, for which we are most grateful.'

Opposite: A group of St Christopher skiers prepare to tackle the slopes during a winter sports trip to Damüls in December 1969.

During the lifespan of any long-standing school, there is the terrible inevitability that it will, at some point, suffer the death of staff and students. On 9 April 1980, Nicholas King Harris was killed in a cycling accident while on holiday with his wife in Gozo. The life of a tremendous individual had come to a sudden end, leaving the school with an absence not easy to fill. An article by Alan Cockburn in the *St Christopher Magazine* reflected that: 'We will remember him as we last saw him, vigorous, kindly and cheerful, as he and Kathleen shook hands with us all in farewell at the end of last Spring Term… He was a good man, who taught by example rather than precept.'

As much as the school was plunged into mourning and remembrance, the energy of its children could never be suppressed. Senior Mistress Mary Muray stepped in as the acting head, assisted by Peter Elbra, head of the Junior School. The school pushed on into a new decade, continuing to build on the foundations laid by a great headmaster.

Overleaf: Self-government in action – the School Council debates a motion, *c.* 1997, with a staff member on his feet making an argument.

FRESH VISIONS 1981–2006

IT IS NEVER EASY TO FOLLOW in the steps of a much-loved headmaster, especially one that had been taken from the post well before his time. Yet such was the task of Colin Reid, who officially adopted the position on 1 January 1981. As with many previous incumbents, Colin brought with him the right mix of educational expertise plus the requisite international outlook. He was a Cambridge historian who had taught in Tonbridge and Nigeria, and was head of History at the United World College of the Atlantic in South Glamorgan. Also in common with many of his predecessors, he joined St Christopher with his own family, having three children with his wife Betsy.

Both as a legacy of Nicholas Harris' work, and under the new governance of Colin Reid, St Christopher's physical development continued apace. From 1980 to 2007, the school was graced with a new hall/theatre complex (in action from September 1982 – a drama festival of eight plays constituted the inaugural productions), a computer room extension to Arunside, an important craft, design and technology (CDT) building, new ICT and English buildings, a cover (at last) plus improved heating for the swimming pool, and substantial renovations to many of the boarding rooms and facilities, to name just some of the projects. The autumn term school magazine also noted that £7,500 had been raised for the Nicholas King Harris Memorial Fund, some of the proceeds going to 'furnishing the Quiet Room' plus investing in curtains for the theatre and a trampoline for the sports hall.

Below: Colin Reid, headmaster of St Christopher between 1981 and 2004.

The newly covered pool brought a level of comfort not experienced by the hardened students of Nicholas Harris's era.

The impressive interior of the new CDT block, showing the near-industrial quality of equipment available to the students.

Students cooking in the Vegetarian Centre. St Christopher has been an almost exclusively vegetarian school since its foundation.

Another interesting addition, in keeping with one of the long-standing school traditions, was the development of the Vegetarian Centre in the early 1980s. The centre focused on the skills of vegetarian cookery, and once opened it established an annual Parents' Circle dinner. Through its innovation and attention to quality, the centre garnered some interest from television – in the spring of 1984 the BBC2 programme *Vegetarian Kitchen* filmed part of its programme in the centre, St Christopher yielding six minutes of air time. In 1989 the school produced a recipe book, entitled *A Square Meal* (actually its second such publication – the first was *Cornucopia* in 1974). The book not only included student and staff recipes but also featured celebrity contributions from the likes of Paul McCartney, Yehudi Menuhin, Tony Benn and the Prince of Wales. Proceeds from sales of it went to Oxfam and to school projects.

The archives of the *St Christopher Magazine* provide a fascinating insight into the cultural and educational life of the school in the 1980s, 1990s and early 2000s. Not only do the magazines reveal the sheer diversity of interests, clubs, activities and achievements within the school, they also, naturally, reflect the mood and concerns of the age.

The school magazine had been through a mix of formats and content choices over the course of its existence. It was edited by senior pupils (or, on occasions, an editorial board) and was largely written by the students themselves, with some contributions from the staff and the head. By the

View of the school in March 1992, by which stage the first phase of the arts block development had been completed but not the second phase.

1980s, it had established a high reputation for the quality of both its production and its writing. Indeed, back in 1950 the *Times Educational Supplement* had said: 'Superbly printed on fine quality paper, the spring issue [of the magazine] contains scraperboard and line drawings of an unusually high standard, and its prose and poems are in the best sense progressive... School editors everywhere would profit by studying the St Christopher technique.'

Looking at just one issue of the magazine – spring 1986 – shows that the praise of 1950s was warranted in the 1980s. The magazine reveals the full spectrum of school life. Running to thirty-four pages in length, it opens with all the latest school news, noting the refurbishment and extension of Arundale, the school's involvement in the Education 2000 computer project, the comings and goings of staff and various pupil trips and outdoor pursuits. A 'Reports' section makes notes on the activities of various school groups, sports teams and societies, such as the Industrial Society's conference in December ('the tasks set range from taking the role of a managing director to taking on the role of a trade union member') and an excursion to the Ashmolean Museum by art enthusiasts. Much of the extent, however, is devoted to creative or reflective poetry and essays, augmented by artworks and photo montages. The contributions come from across the school's students, juniors and seniors, and themes include religion, the beauty of trees, mortality and the school week. The play of ideas is expressive

The school has had regular visitations from professional musicians. Here a violinist from the Fitzwilliam Quartet provides invaluable tuition, c. 2003.

and expansive, reflecting the diversity of intellectual and physical activity in the school.

What is clear from this one magazine was the extent to which activism had become important to the student body. One article in the magazine rails against cruelty to animals, making its point through some graphic images. The article ends with the insistent message: 'This must be stopped.' Yet animal rights was not the only concern. The magazine notes that:

> Due to considerable strength of feeling about the situation of political prisoners overseas, the school Amnesty International group was re-established this term and has gained much support from pupils in virtually all the years of the senior school. Other than its regular letter-writing sessions the group's enterprises included a sponsored silence (organised for the 5 March) and a fund-raising concert performed in conjunction with the school's branch of Youth CND at the end of the Spring term.

As we can see, human rights and nuclear weaponry were hot topics amongst the students of 1989, and such threads continue to this day.

Although youth activism was common across Britain during the 1980s, the students of St Christopher also had opportunities to experience the reality of life amongst less-fortunate communities. In May 1990, for example, the school launched its Rajasthan Project, a scheme for sending older pupils to rural India to work on development schemes amongst poor communities. This was no gentle exchange programme – the students would see poverty first-hand, but also the benefits of practical aid. An article

Opposite top: Typical St Christopher boarding accommodation for Sixth Formers at Arundock during the 1980s. Boarders generally found the eventual transition to university a straightforward experience.

Opposite middle: A Junior School student gets to grips with a BBC Micro computer in the early 1980s – the technology was cutting edge for the time.

Opposite bottom: Members of Arunwood House planting a bower on Arunwood lawn.

Students embrace the great outdoors as part of the Duke of Edinburgh Award Gold practice expedition in 2007.

in the school magazine of summer 1994, written by Steve Anson, explained that no model for such activity existed at the time it was implemented. He also proudly acknowledged that 'some 20% of all St Christopher Sixth Formers spend some time in India between the ages of 16 to 19.' He persuasively explained the benefits of the scheme as a tool for raising awareness and knowledge back at St Christopher:

> In the classroom Rajasthan is often the example we use to teach about a range of issues such as the Environment and Conservation, Economic Awareness, Health, Self Development, International Understanding and Global Citizenship. The project encourages opportunities in almost all curriculum areas, and has been used to enhance appreciation of Art, Geography, Science and Technology. Its value as a teaching tool is immense and it is important that the link can be maintained by future generations of students, teachers and parents of St Chris.

Based on the last sentence here, the writer need not have been concerned – student visits to Rajasthan continue to this day.

The spirit of assistance was not just directed towards international projects. The magazine also notes that the school 'has a long tradition of both community service and learning by doing', citing examples such as visiting old people's homes and local children's homes. The Handicapped Children's Holiday continued – a magazine article from 1984 noted that since its establishment in 1967 the holiday had only missed one year.

Betsy's Bee Club,
c. 1997. Colin
Reid's wife Betsy
taught pupils how
to keep bees as
one of the school
activities.

At the back of the *St Christopher Magazine*, we typically find information regarding the activities of various societies and guilds in the school. In fact, the title of 'Guild' had returned by the 1980s, and a correspondent from 1989 notes, in reference to the original purpose of the guilds:

> In now reviving the title of Guild it is hoped to rediscover this early spirit. The Guilds may go some way towards balancing today's prevalent culture of individualism with a sense of community through shared experiences, so that pride in the school and oneself is excited and developed in the individual, who is part of a sharing and caring community.

SCHOOL GUILDS, 1989
The school magazine for 1989 lists no fewer than five guilds:

The Pottery Guild – dedicated to learning the skills of potting, and selling the products to pupils, parents and others.

The Land Guild – involved in landscaping activities, including establishing a vegetable garden.

The Construction Guild – undertaking light building 'contracts' for school departments; projects included creating student under-bed storage, refurbishing cloakrooms and constructing a cycle shed.

The Baking Guild – baking savoury and sweet foods for sale.

Painting and Decorating Guild – teaching children the skills of painting and decorating, and applying them to school projects.

Field research has always formed an integral part of St Christopher science. Here we see students working on a beach during a biology field trip, 2003.

The revival of the guilds reflects a new awareness of communal commercialism and work experience amongst the student body during the 1980s. For example, in the spring of 1984 members of V and VI Group founded Heads Inc./the Young Enterprise Company, created with the purpose of understanding how small businesses work. Through its board meetings, conducted at the Letchworth Garden City Business Centre, the company decided to produce and sell (within the school and Letchworth town) T-shirts, floor cushions, duvet braces (quickly abandoned) and plant-pot holders. It also looked to market 'an electrical device to inform the driver of a car that his headlights are on'. Reports about the group show a flurry of industry, but unfortunately the team learned some hard lessons about production and cash flow, and went into liquidation by the summer. The managing director, Vickey Hartley, was philosophical: 'Now that the company has gone into liquidation, we can look on the experience as very interesting although I would not advise anyone to partake unless they are totally committed to the idea of making money and will stick with the company through the rough and the smooth of the business world'.

In addition to the guilds and other commercial efforts, the school's societies kept St Christopher's cultural and sporting life at a lively boil. Musical and theatrical output remained extremely high and diverse, while outdoor activities were sustained by groups such as the Sailing Club and Orienteering Club (who in 1987 were filmed by London Weekend Television for a programme on orienteering in Epping Forest). The tradition of the Morning Walk continued, a magazine correspondent arguing for its abolition

– 'All one does is get up at the crack of dawn and walk around a block, which provokes illnesses and colds.'

In the summer of 2003, Colin announced to the school that the Board of Governors were seeking a new head, with he and his wife planning to retire in 2004. When he took over the school, there were 400 pupils. When he left, there were more than 600, a huge expansion. Despite some evident student fears about growth making the school less friendly and encouraging, this does not seem to have occurred.

From 2004 to 2007 the new head was Donald Wilkinson, formerly the principal of Jerodung International School in Brunei. This period was not one of the happiest in St Christopher's history. For a multitude of reasons, such as changes in the system of self-government and in admissions policy, staff and student morale dropped significantly. In the autumn term of 2006, Donald announced his resignation. The school dearly needed a positive force to rekindle its spirit.

Overleaf: The addition of a school climbing wall brought the world of outdoor adventure pursuits directly amongst the school buildings.

Colin Reid and Joan Goodall, long-time housemother of Arunwood, unveil a plaque after the renovation of the Arunwood building, the inscription attesting to a famous former resident.

55

THE OLD AND THE NEW

IN TAKING THE STORY OF St Christopher up to the present day, we maintain the themes of continuity and change that we have witnessed throughout this history. The staff and pupils of the school have always had to walk the line between adapting to the modern age and yet retaining valuable traditions. Leaning purely to one side or the other can lead to either ossification or revolution, neither of which might be best for the student body. St Christopher appears to have walked that balance largely successfully, keeping what is best of the past while allowing the future to lead it onward.

Richard Palmer's connections with St Christopher reached back into his late teens, well before he took up the headship in January 2007. During a gap year he worked at St Christopher helping to set up a design and technology workshop (Richard acknowledges that this brief encounter with St Christopher caused him to 'fall in love' with the school). He then embarked on his academic education (a degree in education from Nottingham Trent) and a diverse career in teaching, specialising in science, drama and CDT. His work took him through a broad range of organisations and contexts, from working for an educational charity through to running a prep school boarding house. However, in 2004 he was appointed head of the Junior School at St Christopher, and this became the stepping-stone to his school headship in 2007.

From the outset, Richard brought a positive new spirit to the school. Following Donald's resignation, he announced his appointment at a Senior School Morning Talk

Richard Palmer, headmaster of St Christopher School since January 2007.

While English, maths and science are compulsory at GCSE, the St Christopher curriculum reflects a broad range of subject interests, including media studies.

on 29 September. The Old Scholars' Club newsletter records: 'He [Richard] told the pupils that they all had their part to play, that schools were about people, not buildings, and that it was a privilege to be asked to be Head, for a while, of this very special school… He said that he would be around at break and lunchtime and invited pupils to come and seek him out and talk to him, adding that he'd look a bit daft on his own.' This message of openness brought a spontaneous round of applause from the students.

It is clear from his writings, and from interviews with the author, that Richard looks back as well as forward in his thinking about the school and its development:

> When the school was founded in 1915, the *Daily Herald* reported that the school was based 'not on the sameness of children, their conformity to type, but on their differences.' This concept of treating children as individuals was revolutionary at the time and continues to be one of the distinctive characteristics of a St Christopher education. We do things differently because they work. We allow children to decide what they wear

The Music Centre features a dedicated music technology suite, as well as more traditional tools, such as these percussion instruments.

to school because it teaches them to be self-reliant and to make informed choices. Everyone is called by their first names (pupils and teaching staff alike) because we have found that this promotes better relationships between children and teachers, based on mutual trust. Parents also tell us that the use of first names makes conversations easier and more productive.

In essence, Richard outlines the creative philosophy behind the original concept for the school. It was this philosophy that has enabled the school to adapt successfully to changing times, including two world wars, several periods of economic depression and numerous changes in national educational policy.

Yet as we have seen, investment in the physical structure of the school has always proved critical to its intellectual expansion. The period from 2007 to the present has been no exception in this regard. A key event was the establishment of an Early Years Centre in Arunwood in 2008–09. By 2007 Arunwood had lapsed into disuse and required substantial redevelopment for its new purpose. The Montessori had been based in Arunfield for many years, on the ground floor of the head's house. Today this space is used as a conference centre, as Arunwood was totally refurbished and refitted as a purpose-built Montessori nursery school. The reception class was also moved into the building in 2012 to form an Early Years Centre.

For its formal opening in September 2009, the children's author Sarah Dyer attended (she is most well known for her popular book *Five Little Fiends*). The focus of the centre is very much that of learning through play, with easy movement for the pupils between the indoors and outdoors.

Other major developments included the creation of a Sixth Form boarding house in Arunside. Richard remembers: 'I wanted the Sixth Form

In both the Junior and Senior Schools at St Christopher, the emphasis remains on finding the students' own learning styles, until they can confidently interact with their environment.

Skateboarding presents something of a health and safety nightmare, but the addition of a skate park was welcomed by most senior boys.

St Christopher has developed a purpose-built theatre and fully equipped dance and drama studio, enabling it to stage professional-level performances.

boarding house to be a bit more independent, and more homely, than it was when the Sixth Form were based in the centre of the school. We weren't using Arunside for anything, and we really wanted to make Sixth Form boarding more attractive.' In addition, we saw in the previous chapter how cookery had taken a prominent place in the school during the 1980s and 1990s. This focus sadly lapsed in the early 2000s, and the Cookery Centre (previously known as the Vegetarian Centre) was abandoned and turned into a boarders' common room. Richard reversed this trend, and the Cookery Centre was re-established in 2011, the buildings and facilities extensively modernised and used for teaching both St Christopher students and pupils from local schools. These three major developments were substantial investments for the school, each costing in the region of £1 million.

The modern St Christopher, after decades of redevelopment, is a world away from those first buildings of 1915. Taking a birds' eye view of the site, it is noticeable how much of the area remains devoted to green open spaces, particularly the playing fields and gardens around Arunfield, Arunside and Arunwood. The theme of outdoor pursuits is touched upon even in the more densely built up areas of the school. Just outside the Junior School Hall, for example, is an official 'Climbing Tree', so the children can indulge in that most timeless of pursuits. At the opposite side of the school is a skate park for the Senior School students (at least those who have parental permission to use it). There is also a climbing wall on one face of the modern languages and geography building.

The rest of the school is state of the art. The purpose-built CDT building not only contains all the tools for practical crafts – from furniture-making to electronics – but also a computer-aided manufacturing area. The Music Department is well stocked with all manner of musical instruments and recording equipment, spawning numerous student music groups, including orchestras, jazz bands and vocal ensembles. Those engaged in sciences have access to fully stocked laboratories, and languages students can use advanced IT software to develop their language skills.

Of course, it is a school's students, not its facilities, that distinguish whether it has been a success or not. Refreshingly, the last decade of student activity – as reflected in the school magazine – continues the trends of creativity and commitment seen through the school's

West Side Story,
2009.

Dance show, 2011.

Oliver!, 2012.

A high-fashion item in the Art Department. The school art gallery shows a range of exceptional talent in diverse media.

history. The School Council, for example, continues to legislate on issues. Its current system, and the reasoning behind it, is here explained more fully by Richard Palmer:

Our Self-Government system is an important part of the School, empowering pupils to play an active role in School life and giving them an early taste of democracy in action. The system is run by a group of elected 'Major Officials'. These are students in the Lower Sixth who run the various committees. The Council is made up of one Councillor from each Company. Anyone may attend Council meetings and put forward motions for discussion but only Councillors may vote. Proposals passed by Council are discussed at a meeting of the entire Senior School, chaired by the Head Boy and Head Girl. A vote is taken and it is the responsibility of the Major Officials to ensure that resolutions passed in a School meeting are enacted. While the Head does have a power of veto, it has been used only five times in the past 25 years.

The longevity of the self-government system is a testament to its success. It is by no means total government by students – the head, staff and governors still control the major policies regarding finance, health and safety, and the curriculum – but it does give the students a vested interest in how their own school is run.

The creative output of the students has remained extremely high over the past decade. A brief walk around the Arts Department, for example, shows exceptionally mature artwork across all forms of media, from life studies to Computer-Generated Imagery (CGI). The school magazine continues to display written work of a high standard, and dozens of former pupils have gone on to careers in art, design and journalism.

Internationalism has also remained at the fore of the school life. As well as regular visits to France, Spain (both as part of language exchange visits), Finland, and the Swiss Alps, St Christopher students continue to make work trips to Rajasthan and Ladakh. One student, Isobel Dunnicliffe, commented on her time in Rajasthan in 2008: 'I feel that I have developed more self-confidence. I was able to stand up and take charge of a large group of children. I also feel now that I am much more decisive... The trip has given me skills which I will carry with me for the rest of my life.' In 2004 the school also established the Kosovo Youth Education Project, running programmes of music, drama, art and sport with Kosovan high-school students. Historical trips have also been arranged, such as visits to battlefields in Normandy.

Having such a lengthy history, St Christopher naturally now has a prodigious community of former students. Many of these students have gone on to distinguished high-profile careers in every conceivable vocation. Former students include actor and presenter Gavin Campbell, journalist/restaurant critic A. A. Gill, golfer Neil Coles, author Jonathan Croall, Whitesnake bass guitarist Neil Murray, publisher Paul Hamlyn, film producer Michael Winner, comedian Olly Mann and theatre producer Sonia Friedman. The school keeps its links to past students via its old scholars' association, the St Christopher Club. Through biannual newsletters, a website, reunions and other events, the club connects a vast and ever-expanding network of memories and friendships.

The proof of a school's worth can often be found in the memories of its former students. Here alumna Sally Janes recounts what her time at the school means after the passage of years:

> The six years I spent at St Chris were very special years, with lots of fantastic memories. I realised just how amazing my schooling had been when I started university and heard about the other students' education. My school days were so enjoyable, providing a well-rounded education, encouraging interests outside of the formal academic education and bringing academic subjects to life. I also made friends for life. Thanks to my parents and St Chris, I grew to be a confident, self-assured individual, with a drive and zest for life. My ambition was to be a journalist and I was able to get a place on a much sought-after journalism course, working part-time at national newspapers and broadcasting companies at the same time to gain experience. After graduating I went to work for the biggest-selling national newspaper. I then went to work for various national newspapers and magazines, before going freelance. I'm married to Rick whom I met at university and we have two young boys. My time at St Chris gave me the confidence to be all I could be, both personally and in my career.

There is a feeling of expansiveness in this statement, the sense that the school delivered character and confidence as much as an education. Such memories are also representative, repeated across thousands of lives. Richard Palmer should have the last word:

> We have been pioneering a distinctive and innovative approach to education for almost 100 years and our methods have stood the test of time. We believe – and universities and employers tell us – that it produces well-rounded, high-capability individuals with the skills and confidence to thrive in the modern world. We can think of no better role for a school.

INDEX